Structural Wonders

Taj Mahal

Christine Webster

Published by Weigl Publishers Inc.
350 5th Avenue, Suite 3304, PMB 6G
New York, NY 10118-0069

Website: www.weigl.com

Library of Congress Cataloging-in-Publication Data

Webster, Christine.
  Taj Mahal / Christine Webster.
      p. cm. -- (Structural wonders)
  Includes index.
  ISBN 978-1-59036-729-2 (hard cover : alk. paper) -- ISBN 978-1-59036-730-8 (soft cover :
alk. paper)
  1. Taj Mahal (Agra, India)--Juvenile literature. 2. Architecture, Mogul--India--Agra--Juvenile
literature. 3. Agra (India)--Buildings, structures, etc.--Juvenile literature. I. Title.
  NA6008.A33W44 2008
  726'.809542--dc22
                          2007012126

Printed in the United States of America
1 2 3 4 5 6 7 8 9 0 11 10 09 08 07

Photograph Credits
Every reasonable effort has been made to trace ownership and to obtain
permission to reprint copyright material. The publishers would be pleased
to have any errors or omissions brought to their attention so that they may
be corrected in subsequent printings.

All of the internet URLs given in the book were valid at the time of publication.
However, due to the dynamic nature of the Internet, some addresses may have
changed, or sites may have ceased to exist since publication. While the author
and publisher regret any inconvenience this may cause readers, no responsibility
for any such changes can be accepted by either the author or the publisher.

Project Coordinators: Heather C. Hudak, Heather Kissock
Design: Terry Paulhus

Contents

5 What is the Taj Mahal?
6 Building History
9 Big Ideas
10 Profile
12 The Science Behind
    the Building
14 Science and Technology
16 Computer-Aided Design
19 Measuring the Taj Mahal
20 Environmental Viewpoint

22 Construction Careers
24 Notable Structures
26 Buildings of Worship
28 Quiz
29 Test the Strength of an Arch
30 Further Research
31 Glossary
32 Index

What is the Taj Mahal?

Structures have been constructed for thousands of years. A structure is a type of building, home, monument, or tower. Some structures are so beautiful that they are famous. The white-marbled Taj Mahal is one of these.

The Taj Mahal is located in Agra, India, on the bank of the Yamuna River. It is a mausoleum, or a type of building that is used as a monument. In a mausoleum, the monument encloses the burial site or tomb of a loved one. In the case of the Taj Mahal, the entire mausoleum is decorated with **calligraphy**, precious jewels, and carvings.

The Taj Mahal consists of a main gateway, gardens, a **mosque**, tomb, and other buildings. The main dome of the structure rises more than 200 feet (61 meters) in the air. Four minarets make up the four corners of the structure. Minarets are tall, tower-like structures often built around mosques.

The Taj Mahal was built because of a great love. A grief-stricken emperor named Shah Jahan built the Taj Mahal to house the grave of his wife, Mumtaz Mahal. The words *Taj Mahal* mean "Crown Palace."

Today, the Taj Mahal is considered to be one of the Seven Wonders of the Modern World. These are structures that are known all over the world for their unique construction.

Quick Bites
- It is believed that when the Taj Mahal was complete, Shah Jahan ordered the architect to be blindfolded. Then, the Shah cut off the architect's hand so he could build no other structure like the Taj Mahal.
- More than three million people visit the Taj Mahal each year.

Building History

India was once controlled by **Muslim** rulers known as the Mughals. Shah Jahan was a Mughal emperor. As emperor, he chose several wives. His favorite wife was named Arjumand Banu Begum. She was from Persia, which is present-day Iran. Shah Jahan called her *Mumtaz Mahal*, which meant "beloved ornament of the palace." He loved Mumtaz dearly.

Mumtaz Mahal and Shah Jahan had 14 children together. After the birth of their fourteenth child, however, Mumtaz became ill and died. Shah Jahan was devastated. He ordered everyone in India into mourning for two years. To honor his wife, he decided to build her the greatest mausoleum on Earth.

Artists were not allowed to paint a royal woman. Paintings of Mumtaz Mahal are based on descriptions.

Building the Taj Mahal took a great deal of planning. Shah Jahan was so rich that any resource was available to him. Architects, builders, and artisans flocked to Agra. They offered designs for the magnificent tomb that used Hindu, Persian, and Mughal architectural ideas and would be constructed of red sandstone.

Some believe that Shah Jahan was going to build an identical, black-marble mausoleum on the other side of the river. It was to house Shah Jahan after his death.

TIMELINE OF CONSTRUCTION

January 15, 1592: Shah Jahan is born.

1593: Mumtaz Mahal is born as Arjumand Banu Begum.

1612: Shah Jahan marries Mumtaz Mahal.

1627: Shah Jahan becomes emperor. He gives his wife the title of Mumtaz Mahal.

1631: Mumtaz dies following childbirth.

1632: Construction of the Taj Mahal, Mumtaz Mahal's tomb, begins.

1643: The mausoleum and some of the surrounding buildings are completed.

1653: The rest of the surrounding buildings and garden are completed.

1666: Shah Jahan dies and is buried next to Mumtaz Mahal.

1861: The archaeological survey is created to preserve monuments of India and to restore the Taj Mahal and other Agra buildings.

About 114,000 cartloads of red sandstone were used to build the gate and foundation of the Taj Mahal.

Such designs were common, and Shah Jahan wanted the Taj Mahal to be unique. He wanted to build the entire structure out of white marble. He also planned to decorate it with expensive jewels.

Aurangzeb was the last great Mughal emperor. He reigned from 1658 to 1707.

Construction of the Taj Mahal complex began in 1632 and took more than 20 years to complete. When the Taj Mahal was completed, Shah Jahan often went there to worship his wife. In 1657, however, he became ill, and his life took another turn. The Shah's son, Aurangzeb, wanted to take over his father's position as emperor. Taking advantage of his father's illness, Aurangzeb plotted to take over his father's throne. He put his ill father under house arrest at the Red Fort, the ruler's palace in Agra.

With Shah Jahan locked away at the Red Fort, Aurangzeb officially declared himself emperor in 1658. Shah Jahan eventually died—eight years after the Taj had been completed. Aurangzeb buried Shah Jahan next to Mumtaz Mahal.

A rear view of the Taj Mahal can be seen from the Yamuna River.

Big Ideas

Mausoleums have been built since the beginning of time. Emperors, kings, and even regular people build them to honor their loved ones. Shah Jahan wanted to build the world's greatest mausoleum to show how deeply he loved his wife. After her death, he had little interest in ruling the land, and instead, focused his attention on art and architecture.

Word of the mausolem quickly spread across the land. Highly skilled mathematicians and engineers came from far and wide to help with the concept. The concept involved constructing an entire complex around the mausoleum, the Taj Mahal.

Six months after his wife's death, Shah Jahan laid the foundation of the Taj Mahal. To put the concept into place, he first had to choose a site. He chose an area on the bank of the Yamuna River, near his palace in Agra.

The Taj Mahal stands at the far end of the 42-acre grounds. It has four, nearly identical sides, each with a wide central **arch** and several smaller arches. At the top, there is a central dome and four smaller domes. A minaret stands at each of the four corners of the base of the Taj Mahal. The tomb is located inside the Taj Mahal. A four-part garden includes reflecting pools, footpaths, fountains, and trees. Two identical, red sandstone buildings were constructed on the northeastern and northwestern sides of the garden. Facing east is the mosque. The rest house faces west. A red sandstone and marble gate adorns the southern end of the complex.

Web Link:
To find out more about the gardens of the Mughal Empire, visit www.mughalgardens.org.

1) The mosque, or *Masjid*, stands to the west of the Taj Mahal. 2) The marble of the Taj Mahal appears to be slightly different colors thoughout the day, depending on the sunlight. 3) Walls surround the Taj Mahal complex.

Profile:

Architects and designers of the Taj Mahal

It is not known who actually designed the Taj Mahal. Architects from around the world, including Persia, India, Italy, and the **Ottoman Empire** were called upon to help create the structure. However, a man named Ustad Isa is most often noted as the main designer of the Taj Mahal.

Ustad Isa was an architect, mathematician, and astronomer. Some historians believe that Ustad was the architect of the Red Fort, Shah Jahan's palace.

Other people believe that an Italian named Geronimo Veroneo designed the Taj Mahal. In 1640, a monk visited Agra and met Veroneo. He wrote that Veroneo was responsible for the design. There is little evidence to support this claim, however. The real identity of the designer is still unknown.

Many **artisans** helped make the Taj Mahal beautiful. Ismail Khan designed the main dome of the Taj Mahal. He was from the Ottoman Empire and was considered one of the best designers of domes in that era.

MUGHAL ARCHITECTURE

Red Fort, Dehli, India
The Dehli Fort is also known as the Red Fort. This fort was built between 1638 and 1648. It was used as the palace for the Mughal Empire. The fort was built with tons of red sandstone blocks. Its walls are 1.5 miles (2.5 kilometers) long and have heights of 60 feet (18 meters) to 110 feet (34 m).

Agra Fort, Agra, India
The Agra Fort was built in 1565 and is located about 1.5 miles (2.5 km) from the Taj Mahal. It is a city that is completely enclosed in walls. The Agra Fort is much larger than the Red Fort in Dehli.

Ali Mardan Khan, a Persian engineer, is believed to have prepared and cleared the construction site. Amanat Khan, also from Persia, was the main calligrapher. His name is inscribed on the gateway to the Taj Mahal. Muhammad Hanif was the chief **mason**. Amir Ali was a master stonecutter. He gave his expertise in designing the bricks that make up the **foundation** and walls of the Taj Mahal. Chiranji Lal was the main sculptor and the person who designed the **mosaic**. Qazim Khan was responsible for the solid gold ornament on top of the dome.

There were a number of senior artisans on the creative team, including 37 stonecutters. However, another 20,000 workers were needed to complete the structure.

The Taj Mahal complex cost 32 million rupees to build. This is equal to about $740,000 U.S. dollars.

Shalimar Gardens

The Shalimar Gardens were built in 1641 by Shah Jahan. The gardens measure 2,159 feet by 847 feet (658 m by 258 m). They feature 410 fountains and five water cascades. The gardens are located near Lahore City in Pakistan.

Tomb of Jahangir

This mausoleum was built in 1637 and is located in Lahore, Pakistan. Jahangir was a Mughal Emperor and Shah Jahan's father. He ruled from 1605 to 1627. Shah Jahan built this mausoleum for his father. It is featured on the Pakistani bank note.

The Science Behind the Building

A monument such as the Taj Mahal needed the strongest materials. It also needed a design that was indestructible. Shah Jahan designed the Taj Mahal using ancient scientific principles that are still used.

The Properties of Marble

Marble is known as a soft rock. This means that it can be easily cut and shaped. The measurement of hardness scale (MOHS) determines the hardness of a stone based on how easily it can be scratched by grit or hard objects. On this scale, marble is a three out of ten. A hard piece of plastic rates about 2 on this scale. It could not scratch marble. However, quartz, which measures 7, will scratch marble. Marble's softness allows the rock to be sculpted into beautiful artistic shapes by creating grooves and straight edges. It is often used for sculpting and building.

Shah Jahan chose marble because of its availability, its texture, and its beauty. India has a vast supply of marble in the country. The Taj Mahal's marble came from a nearby town called Makrana. The marble used is called Makrana marble.

Steel columns and beams form a three-dimensional grid in the structure of the building.

Strength in Form

The Taj Mahal was built stone by stone. Bricks had to be laid in such a way that would give the building the greatest strength as a whole. To create this strength, the marble stones of the Taj were layered on top of each other in a pattern. Each rectangular block of marble was about 15 to 18 inches (38 to 46 centimeters) thick. One stone was placed lengthwise. Another stone was placed beside the first with its short end facing outward. The pattern repeated on each row and layer. Each brick was **fused** with a mixture of lime **mortar**. Iron clamps held the blocks in place. Once the mortar mixture dried, the clamps were removed. This system of long and short slabs helped support the heavy walls. It also stopped stones from coming loose later on.

Arches

Arches have been used to support structures since 300 BC. Above its foundation, the Taj Mahal is supported by arched **vaults**. By building an archway, heavy weights can be supported. The weight of a structure presses downward. With an arch, this is changed from a downward force to an outward force. The outward force spreads the weight of the structure evenly across a larger area. Ancient arches are built from stone. Today, they can be constructed from wood, concrete, wire, and brick.

Web Link:
To find out more about how arches work, visit http://science.how stuffworks.com/bridge5.htm.

Science and Technology

Building the Taj Mahal was a long and difficult process. The workers did not have the technology found in the world today. People had to use the technology that was available to them at the time.

Ramps and Scaffolding

When the Taj Mahal was built, the workers relied on ramps and scaffolding to lift heavy slabs of marble. A ramp is a type of simple machine called an inclined plane. A plane is a flat surface. When it is slanted, or inclined, at an angle other than a right angle, it can help move objects across distances. Using a relatively small force, one can move a large resistance, such as marble. Ten-mile (16-km) ramps made from packed earth were built throughout the city and led up to the building. To build the ramps, earth was spread in layers. It was tamped down and packed tightly before another layer of earth was added. This process of layering and tamping created a stable ramp that would not fall apart. Elephants and oxen dragged slabs of marble along the ramp. Teams of 30 oxen would pull the marble blocks. It took more than five years to move the materials to the site using these ramps. The building, however, continued to be constructed while the materials were being transported.

As the building grew in height, brick scaffolding was built. Scaffolding is like a ladder. It has platforms at each level and

Scaffolding is still used in construction today.

Chisels can be used to shape wood as well as stone.

is easy to climb. The platforms provided the workers with a stable work area. When one area is complete, another level of scaffolding was added.

Pulleys

To help lift heavy items, workers used pulleys and ropes. A pulley is a wheel with a groove along the edge. This groove holds a rope in place. One end of the rope is attached to the load being moved. The other end is pulled by a human or an animal. The pulley eases the weight of the load so that the object is easier to lift. A treadwheel is a type of pulley system that is used to lift heavy objects. Two people stand inside the wooden wheel beside one another. They walk along the wheel to make it turn around the **shaft**. This winds ropes through a pulley system that raises or lowers the load.

Chisels and Crowbars

To create the Taj Mahal, thousands of blocks of marble needed to be cut from mountainsides. To do this, workers used iron chisels to cut grooves into the marble. Then, they placed wooden wedges into the grooves and filled the grooves with water. This soaked the wood, causing it to expand. With the expansion, the marble was forced to crack. A wedge is a type of simple machine. It is used to push things apart by converting motion on one direction into a splitting motion at the other end. The splitting occurs at right angles to the blade. Using another simple tool, an iron crowbar, the workers then pried the blocks of marble away from the mountain. A crowbar is a type of lever. It has an arm that pivots, or turns, around a **fulcrum**. The curved arm of the crowbar rests against the surface. As it is rotated, it pries the object away from the surface.

Quick Bites
- More than 1,000 elephants were used to transport materials to the Taj Mahal site.
- It is believed that the scaffolding and labor actually cost as much as the entire Taj Mahal. At one point, the scaffolding enclosed the entire tomb. It should have taken five years just to dismantle. However, legend says that Shah Jahan told the workers that if they took down the scaffolding, they could keep the bricks. It was dismantled overnight.

Computer-Aided Design

Architects are trained professionals who work with clients to design structures. Before anything is built, they make detailed drawings or models. These plans are important tools that help people visualize what the structure will look like. A blueprint is a detailed diagram that shows where all the parts of the structure will be placed. Walls, doors, windows, plumbing, electrical wiring, and other details are mapped out on the blueprint. Blueprints act as a guide for engineers and builders during construction.

For centuries, architects and builders worked without the aid of computers. Sketches and blueprints were drawn by hand. Highly skilled drafters would draw very technical designs. Today, this process is done using computers and sophisticated software programs. Architects use CAD, or computer-aided design, throughout the design process. Early CAD systems used computers to draft building plans. Today's computer programs can do much more. They can build three-dimensional models and computer simulations of how a building will look. They can also calculate the effects of different physical forces on the structure. Using CAD, today's architects can build more complex structures at lower cost and in less time.

Computer-aided design programs have been used since the 1960s.

Eye on Design

Three-Dimensional Virtual Reality Tool

To see inside the Taj Mahal and tour the grounds, go to www.taj-mahal.net, and click on "Explore the Virtual Tour."

Many people visit the Taj Mahal every year. Many more would like to visit, but cannot. Computer technology, in the form of three-dimensional virtual reality, has provided a way for anyone to visit the Taj Mahal with the click of a computer mouse. Two-dimensional technology appears as a flat photograph on computer screens. This means that objects seem to have length and width, but they do not have depth. With three-dimensional technology, objects appear to have depth as well. Three-dimensional technology can be used to provide a 360-degree view of a place. It has been used to provide a unique perspective of the Taj Mahal and its complex.

Using three-dimensional virtual reality, Internet users can catch a glimpse inside the Taj Mahal and other buildings on the complex. By rotating through panoramic views of different areas, visitors will feel as if they are standing in the middle of the Taj Mahal. Vistors can use their computer mouse to move around each area. An overall map of the grounds shows visitors what part of the complex they are viewing.

MEASURING THE TAJ MAHAL

Location

The Taj Mahal complex is in Agra, India, along the bank of the Yamuna River. The Taj Mahal is located 900 feet (274 m) from the main entrance.

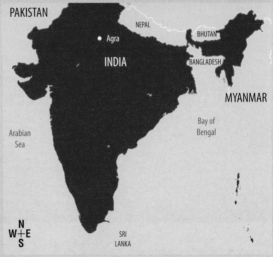

Height

- The main dome is 240 feet (73 m) high.
- The main structure is 186 feet (57 m) high on each side.
- The Taj Mahal consists of four corner minarets. Each is 131 feet (40 m) high.
- The Taj Mahal stands on a raised platform. It is 20 feet high (6.1 m).

Area

The Taj Mahal is set on a square platform. Its four minarets are set on an octagonal base. The garden is rectangular in shape. It is 1,050 feet by 984 feet (320 m x 300 m).

Other Interesting Facts

- More than 40 types of semi-precious and precious jewels were used to decorate the Taj Mahal.
- Each design of a 3-inch (7.6-cm) flower on the Taj Mahal may have up to 70 jewels on one leaf.
- The jewels used on the Taj Mahal came from all over the continent, including countries such as China, Afghanistan, Tibet, Arabia, and Sri Lanka.
- By the 19th century, parts of the Taj Mahal were falling apart from wear. In some places, British soldiers chiseled out the precious stones, ruining the work.
- The Taj Mahal is a World Heritage Site. It is a place of cultural heritage that is being preserved for future generations.

Environmental Viewpoint

The city of Agra was built on the western bank of the Yamuna River in 1475. When the Mughal rulers took over the city, it flourished. Forts, buildings, and tombs were built during this time. Today, millions of people visit India each year. The Taj Mahal has been a main tourist attraction for many years. In fact, 10,000 people visit each day. This has taken a toll on the Taj Mahal.

Many people who visit the building want to touch the smooth marble. This simple gesture is hurting the Taj Mahal. People naturally have oils on their fingertips. Each time they touch the marble, some of the oil is left behind. The oil attracts grime, which eventually **erodes** the marble.

Even breathing is creating problems for the Taj Mahal. Every breath a tourist takes sends moisture into the air. The moisture helps mold grow on the marble. This causes erosion and makes the marble crack. Sometimes, the Taj Mahal is hurt by vandalism. Years of trying to chip the jewels out of the walls have crumbled the marble.

Like any other city, Agra is greatly affected by pollution. The city of Agra is **congested**. Thousands of people make their home here and work in the city. Congested cities crammed with vehicles, people, and factories are harming the Taj Mahal. Thick black smoke from cars and factories sends pollution into the air. As it mixes with moisture, it falls as acid rain. The acid rain **corrodes** the Taj Mahal's marble.

Due to its exposure to the open air, the Taj Mahal is vulnerable to damage from airborne pollution, including car exhaust and factory smoke.

The government of India has banned vehicles that use gas from the area. Instead, battery driven cars or horse- or camel-pulled carts must be used. The government has closed down many factories that send pollutants into the air. They are trying to clean up the Yamuna River. With these efforts, the Taj Mahal may continue to flourish.

A SOLID FOUNDATION

The site of the Taj Mahal was once a floodplain. A floodplain is an area along a river bank that is often flooded with water. To make sure this did not affect the building, the Taj Mahal had to be built on a sturdy platform.

Workers dug channels by the Yamuna River. This widened the river. It rerouted the water so that it would flow beside the Taj Mahal. Then, the workers dug an area more than three football fields in length for the foundation. They dug down until they hit rock and then laid a foundation of stone and lime mortar. The lime mortar cemented the stones together. A thick layer of a chemical mixture was placed overtop to make the foundation waterproof in case the plain flooded again.

Scientists continue to monitor the Taj Mahal's foundation. They fear that the Yamuna River may dry up. This would cause its banks to sink. The Taj Mahal would then tilt. This could cause the structure to deteriorate. Wells were built underneath the structure to keep water away from the foundation.

Today, the northern side of the Taj Mahal is 1.44 inches (3.7 cm) lower than then southern side.

Construction Careers

It takes a large team to build a structure as grand as the Taj Mahal. Although it is not certain who designed it, two men supervised its construction. Mir Abdul Karim and Mukrimat Khan are credited with overseeing the entire project and team. In today's society, they would be considered foremen. They made sure materials arrived on time, consulted plans, looked after finances, and supervised 20,000 workers from numerous professions. Architects, engineers, artists, masons, calligraphers, and laborers made up the Taj Mahal team.

Masons

Brick buildings are built with the help of a mason. A mason is a professional who works with stones or bricks. Masonry is an ancient skill. Building the Taj Mahal required the skills of many masons. When the raw marble slabs arrived at the construction site, each slab had to be shaped and smoothed. Masons used an L-shaped tool called a square to measure the pieces. Each block had to be a specific size. The masons scratched the measurements onto the marble. Then, with a chisel and mallet, they would strike the marble. Once the stone was roughly the right shape, a smaller tool was used to remove tiny edges. This tool was similar to an ice pick with a sharp point. The stone was then shaped into a flat, rectangular block and was polished. The mason slid an iron plate with

coarse or fine sand across the stone. This acted as sandpaper, making the marble smooth as glass. Sometimes, a mason would carve a symbol, or mason's mark, into the marble. This showed others who designed this "piece of art." Today, masons continue to work on buildings. They shape bricks and stones and lay them in place.

Laborers

Laborers were responsible for bringing the marble to the Taj Mahal site. They led teams of oxen over ramps and hauled water from the river. The water was mixed to make mortar to hold the bricks together. Laborers built scaffolding so that there were platforms to build the brick walls higher. They also shimmied over the dome area to lay the bricks. Laborers play an important role on construction teams today. They perform many tasks, including cleaning sites, building concrete forms, loading materials, and operating equipment. Some tasks require special training, while others can be done without experience. However, laborers should be physically fit to do most jobs.

Calligraphers

Calligraphers added their artistry to the Taj Mahal. They used scrolls to inscribe passages into the gate and the walls around the Taj Mahal. Calligraphers specialize in the art of fine handwriting. Calligraphy may be used to decorate buildings or art pieces. It is often used to write wedding and event invitations. There are many different forms of calligraphy, depending on the part of the world, language, or culture that is being presented by the calligrapher.

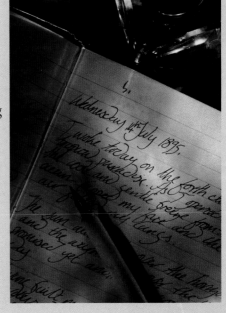

Web Link:
To find out more about laborers, visit www.bls.gov/oco/ocos248.htm.

Notable Structures

Throughout history, people have used stone to build many structures. The ancient Egyptians used stone to construct the Great Pyramids. In Greece, archtitects designed structures such as the Parthenon from marble.

Bibi Ka Maqbara

Built: 1678

Location: Aurangabad, Maharashtra

Design: Prince Azam Shah

Description: Shah Jahan's son, Aurangzeb, built this temple to rival the Taj Mahal. Like his father, Aurangzeb built this mausoleum for his wife— Rabia-ud-Durrani. Aurangzeb's son, Azam Shah, was the designer. It was built at the end of the Mughal reign. It is smaller than the Taj Mahal and cost less to build.

Itmad-Ud-Daulah's Tomb

Built: 1622–1628

Location: Agra, Uttar Pradesh

Design: Nur Jahan

Description: Itmad-Ud-Daulah's Tomb is located on the left side of the Yamuna River. This mausoleum is nicknamed the Baby Taj. Nur Jahan built the tomb for her father, Mirza Ghiyas Beg. As a government official, he was given the name Itmad-Ud-Daulah. He was Mumtaz Mahal's grandfather.

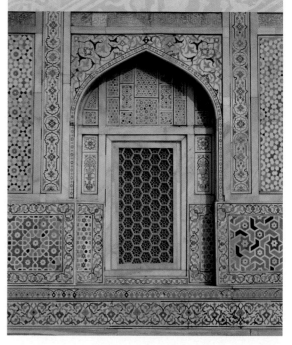

Like the Taj Mahal, these structures are well known around the world. However, there are many other important stone buildings that were constructed in India during the Mughal rule.

Jama Masjid

Built: 1658

Location: Delhi, India

Design: Shah Jahan

Description: The Jama Masjid is a temple, or place of worship, for the people of India. It is the largest mosque in India. It consists of gateways, towers, and two minarets. Each minaret is 131 feet (40 m) high. Visitors may reach the top of the minarets. Here, they can see all of Delhi.

Fatehpur Sikri

Built: 1571

Location: Uttar Pradesh, India

Design: Mughal Emperor Akbar

Description: This World Heritage Site was built in honor of a saint named Salim Chishti. When the Mughals ruled, it was the political capital. Fatehpur Sikri consists of palaces, halls, and mosques. Panch Mahal is located here. This five-story building has 176 carved columns on its bottom floor.

Buildings of Worship

India is not the only place with memorial structures. All over the world, temples and monuments have been constructed for different reasons. Some are tombs. Others are

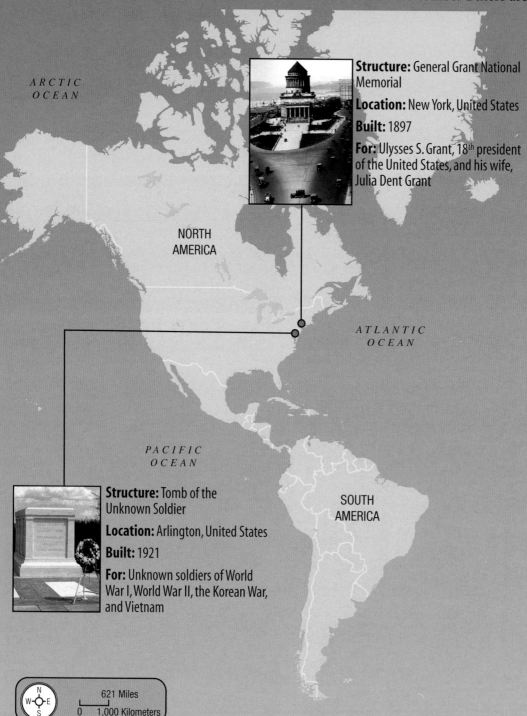

Structure: General Grant National Memorial

Location: New York, United States

Built: 1897

For: Ulysses S. Grant, 18th president of the United States, and his wife, Julia Dent Grant

ARCTIC OCEAN

NORTH AMERICA

ATLANTIC OCEAN

PACIFIC OCEAN

Structure: Tomb of the Unknown Soldier

Location: Arlington, United States

Built: 1921

For: Unknown soldiers of World War I, World War II, the Korean War, and Vietnam

SOUTH AMERICA

N
W E
S

621 Miles

0   1,000 Kilometers

memorials to honor people. This map features just a few of the monuments that have been built around the world.

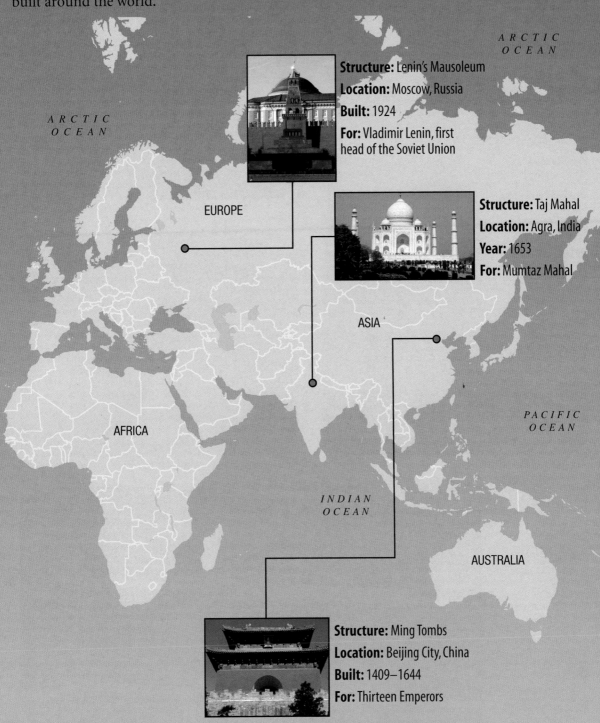

A R C T I C
O C E A N

Structure: Lenin's Mausoleum
Location: Moscow, Russia
Built: 1924
For: Vladimir Lenin, first head of the Soviet Union

A R C T I C
O C E A N

EUROPE

Structure: Taj Mahal
Location: Agra, India
Year: 1653
For: Mumtaz Mahal

ASIA

PACIFIC
OCEAN

AFRICA

INDIAN
OCEAN

AUSTRALIA

Structure: Ming Tombs
Location: Beijing City, China
Built: 1409–1644
For: Thirteen Emperors

Quiz

Q Why was marble chosen to build the Taj Mahal?

A Marble was chosen for its availability, its texture, and its beauty.

Q Why were arches used?

A Arches support extreme weights evenly by changing the downward force of the building to an outward force.

Q Why were the marble slabs placed lengthwise and then widthwise?

A This gave the structure strength. It also prevented the bricks from coming loose.

Q Why was scaffolding used to build the temples?

A Scaffolding provides a level work area. It gives the workers a hands-free environment and lets them work at high heights safely.

Test the Strength of an Arch

Arches are used to support heavy weights. They use minimal materials. They are cost efficient and strong. Arches are also architecturally attractive. Try this activity to see how arches really work.

Materials

- Four eggs
- Heavy books
- Cellophane tape
- Scissors

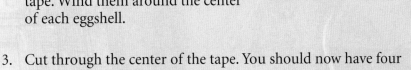

Instructions

1. Break off the smallest end of each egg. Pour the insides into a bowl. Store in fridge to cook or bake with later. Throw out broken ends.

2. Take four long pieces of cellophane tape. Wind them around the center of each eggshell.

3. Cut through the center of the tape. You should now have four dome-shaped shells.

4. Lay the four domes on a table in a rectangle. Make sure the flat side is down.

5. Estimate how many books you can lay across the domes.

6. Now, lay books one by one across the dome. See how many books you can lay down before the shells break.

Further Research

You can find more information on the Taj Mahal and other structures of the world at your local library or on the Internet.

Websites

For more information on the Taj Mahal, visit
www.pbs.org/treasuresoftheworld/a_nav/taj_nav/main_tajfrm.html

For more information on wonders of the world, including the Taj Mahal, visit www.nationalgeographic.com/traveler/tajmahal.html

For more information on ancient Indian temples, visit www.indiantemplesportal.com

Glossary

arch: a curved structure that spans an opening

artisans: craftspeople

calligraphy: a highly decorative type of handwriting

congested: overcrowded or thick

corrodes: eats away

erodes: wears away

foundation: the base on which something stands

fulcrum: the point on which a lever turns

fused: united by melting

mason: a person skilled in building with stone

mortar: a mixture of lime, sand, and water, used as a bond between bricks

mosaic: a decoration made up of small pieces of colored glass or stone

mosque: a Muslim place of worship

Muslim: a follower of the Islamic religion

Ottoman Empire: a former Turkish empire in Europe, Asia, and Africa, which lasted from the late 13th century until the end of World War I

shaft: a revolving rod that transmits motion or power

vaults: arched structures that form a roof or ceiling

Index

acid rain 20
Agra 5, 7, 9, 10, 19, 20, 24, 27
architect 5, 6, 10, 16, 22, 24
Aurangzeb 7

Bibi Ka Maqbara 24

chisel 15
crowbar 15

dome 5, 9, 11, 19, 23

Fatehpur Sikri 25

Isa, Ustad 10
Itmad-Ud-Daulah's Tomb 24

Jama Masjid 25
jewels 5, 7, 19, 20

marble 5, 9, 12, 13, 14, 15, 20, 22, 23, 24, 28
minaret 5, 9, 19, 25
Mughals 6, 9, 10, 20, 24, 25
Mumtaz Mahal 5, 6, 7, 24, 27

Ottoman Empire 10

pollution 20, 21
pulleys 15

ramps 14
Red Fort 7, 10

scaffolding 14, 15, 23, 28
Shah Jahan 5, 6, 7, 11, 12, 15, 24, 25

Veroneo, Geronimo 10

Yamuna River 5, 9, 19, 20, 21, 24